THIS BOOK HAS BEEN WRITTEN FOR INFORMATION PURPOSES ONLY. EVERY EFFORT HAS BEEN MADE TO MAKE

DO YOU POSSESS OR WORK YOUR OWN SITE OR ONLINE BUSINESS? WITH THE RISING NOTORIETY OF THE WEB, THERE IS A DECENT POSSIBILITY THAT YOU DO. WHICHEVER SORT OF SITE YOU HAVE, DID YOU KNOW THAT YOU COULD ASSIST WITH ADVANCING IT WITH ONLINE MEDIA?
I'M CERTAIN LARGE NUMBERS OF YOU HAVE KNOWN ABOUT VARIOUS WEB-BASED MEDIA LOCALES LIKE FACEBOOK, YOUTUBE, TWITTER, MYSPACE, LINKEDIN, BLOGGER

WORDPRESS, AND OTHERS. WITH A GENUINELY HUGE NUMBER OF SUCH
ONLINE MEDIA SITES HAVING NORTH OF A MILLIONS CLIENTS, THERE IS A DECENT POSSIBILITY THAT BY JOINING THESE DESTINATIONS, YOU MAKE NEW COMPANIONS AS WELL AS OBSERVE WEB CLIENTS THAT SOUNDS INSPIRED BY AT LEAST IN THEORY
VISITING YOUR SITE.

SUBSEQUENTLY, BY JOINING THESE WEB-BASED MEDIA LOCALES AND AFTERWARD GIVING A CONNECTION TO YOUR SITE IN THESE DESTINATIONS, YOU OUGHT TO GET VARIOUS NEW GUESTS TO YOUR SITE.ASSUMING YOU HAVE ABSOLUTELY NO INVOLVEMENT IN ONLINE MEDIA OR ON THE OTHER HAND IN THE EVENT THAT YOU ARE AS YET THINKING ABOUT HOW AND WHY YOU SHOULD UTILIZE ONLINE MEDIA TO ADVANCE YOUR SITE, THEN,

WHAT IS SOCIAL MEDIA?
WITH THE BEGINNING OF
NUMEROUS WEB-BASED
BUSINESS OPEN DOORS,
WHICH OFFER AN
OPPORTUNITY FOR
INDIVIDUALS TO
APPRECIATE
MAKING MONEY FROM THE
SOLACES OF THEIR OWN
HOMES, INCREASINGLY
MORE HAVE BECOME
INQUISITIVE
CONCERNING WHAT WEB-
BASED MEDIA TRULY IS
ABOUT, AND THE WAY
THAT IT CAN HELP THEIR
ONLINE BUSINESS
VOCATIONS. FIRST
ALSO CHIEF,

INCREASINGLY MORE HAVE BECOME INQUISITIVE CONCERNING WHAT WEB-BASED MEDIA TRULY IS ABOUT, AND THE WAY THAT IT CAN HELP THEIR ONLINE BUSINESS PROFESSIONS. FIRST WHAT'S MORE PREMIER, ONLINE MEDIA CAN MEAN TWO THINGS. FOR ONE'S PURPOSES, IT VERY WELL MAY BE AN INSTRUMENT THAT IS UTILIZED FOR INDIVIDUALS TO IMPART AND IMPART SPECIFIC THINGS TO THEIR COMPANIONS AND LOVE ONES; AND, IT VERY WELL MAY BE

UTILIZED AS A WEB SHOWCASING PROCEDURE THAT EXPLOITS THE IMPACT OF SOCIAL ORGANIZING LOCALES LIKE FACEBOOK, YOUTUBE, TWITTER, MYSPACE, AND SOME MORE.

AT THE POINT WHEN YOU GET EVERYTHING ROLLING WITH A WEB-BASED BUSINESS, WHICH IS WORKED THROUGH YOUR OWN SITE PAGE, SOMETHING THAT YOU SHOULD ACHIEVE TO SUCCEED IS TO DRIVE A TREMENDOUS VOLUME OF

TRAFFIC TO IT CONSISTENTLY. WEB TRAFFIC JUST MEANS THE QUANTITY OF INDIVIDUALS VISITING YOUR WEB-BASED INTERFACE; AND, PERHAPS THE MOST EFFECTIVE WAY TO DO THAT IS USING WEB-BASED MEDIA PROMOTING. ONE INSTANCE OF EXPLOITING A LONG RANGE INTERPERSONAL COMMUNICATION WEBPAGE

TO ADVANCE YOUR SITE IS BY
PUTTING A CONNECTION TO IT,
STRAIGHTFORWARDLY ON YOUR FACEBOOK RECORD TO BE SEEN BY OTHERS. ALONG THESE LINES, ASSUMING YOU HAVE CURRENTLY DONE THAT, THEN, AT THAT POINT, YOU ENJOY CURRENTLY TAKEN BENEFIT OF ONLINE MEDIA PROMOTING.
ONE REASON WHY EFFECTIVE INTERNET BASED ADVERTISERS UTILIZE WEB-BASED

BASED MEDIA TO
ADVANCE THEIR
ONLINE ORGANIZATIONS
IS THE WAY THAT SUCH
SITES ARE PROFOUNDLY
VISITED BY A GREAT
MANY INDIVIDUALS ON A
CUSTOMARY PREMISE.
WITH FACEBOOK ALONE,
IT REALLY HAS MORE
THAN 500 MILLION
ENLISTED CLIENTS IN A
WORLDWIDE
SCALE. IN THIS MANNER,
THERE IS NO DOUBT THAT
A SPECIFIC LEVEL OF IT
HAS A PLACE WITH YOUR
OBJECTIVE MARKET.

RETURNING TO THAT MODEL, YOU ARE IN REALITY EXPLOITING ONE SITE; IN THIS WAY, IF ADD THE QUANTITIES OF OTHER STRONG ONLINE MEDIA LOCALES REFERENCED ON TOP, THEN, AT THAT POINT, YOU MIGHT BE CAPABLE TO HAVE HUGE NUMBER OF INDIVIDUALS VISITING YOUR SITE WEB-BASED MEDIA IS FOR SURE ONE OF THE MOST IMPRESSIVE INTERNET ADVERTISING TECHNIQUES THAT YOU CAN MAKE UTILIZATION OF.

TO ACQUIRE TRAFFIC TO
YOUR SITE. NONETHELESS,
YOU WANT TO REMEMBER
THAT OUTCOMES
FROM IT MIGHT REQUIRE
SOME INVESTMENT TO GET
FIGURED IT OUT. THIS IS
ON THE GROUNDS THAT
YOU WILL IN ANY CASE
NEED TO FABRICATE YOUR
NOTORIETY
SO THAT AN EVER
INCREASING NUMBER OF
INDIVIDUALS WOULD
FOLLOW YOUR SITE.

CONTINUOUSLY RECALL
HOWEVER THAT
HUGE NUMBER OF
WEBSITE ADMINS CAN
ACQUIRE
ACCOMPLISHMENT FROM
IT, AND SINCE THEY CAN,
YOU OUGHT TO BE
READY TO GET THE
ADVANTAGES FROM IT
ALSO.
TO BEGIN, IT IS IDEAL TO
KNOW THE KINDS OF WEB-
BASED MEDIA
SHOWCASING FIRST.
BESIDE THAT, DO
NOT FAIL TO REMEMBER
THAT

THE MAJORITY OF THESE SITES WERE NOT AT FIRST MADE FOR BUSINESS PURPOSES, HOWEVER AS A METHOD FOR SPANNING HOLES BETWEEN INDIVIDUALS WHO ARE SITUATED A LONG WAY FROM ONE ANOTHER. IN THIS MANNER, YOU REALLY WANT TO FABRICATE CONNECTIONS FIRST, JUST AS ENGAGE INQUIRIES FROM INTRIGUED PEOPLE FROM TIME TO TIME.

VARIOUS TYPES OF SOCIAL MEDIA

ASSUMING YOU ARE GOING TO KICK OFF YOUR ONLINE BUSINESS PROFESSION WITH THE MAKING OF YOUR OWN SITE, YOU SHOULD REALIZE THAT THERE ARE NUMEROUS WEB BASED SHOWCASING METHODOLOGIES THAT YOU REALLY WANT TO UTILIZE, TO ACQUIRE ACHIEVEMENT IN IT. ONE OF WHICH IS ONLINE MEDIA ADVERTISING, AND SOMETHING THAT

YOU REALLY WANT TO DO
TO EXPLOIT IT IS TO KNOW
ITS VARIOUS KINDS.
AS A RULE, THERE ARE
TWO UNIQUE SORTS OF
ONLINE MEDIA TO BE
SPECIFIC OFF-WEBSITE
AND ON LOCATION. BY
KNOWING
THE VARIOUS SORTS OF
ONLINE MEDIA
ADVERTISING, YOU WILL
ACTUALLY WANT TO
KNOW THE APPROPRIATE
ADVANCES THAT YOU
NEED TO EXPLOIT THIS
INTERNET SHOWCASING
PROCEDURE. BESIDE THAT,
YOU WILL

ADDITIONALLY SEE BETTER, WHY SUCH ADVANCES ARE TAKEN TO HELP YOUR OWN SITE. OFF-WEBPAGE ONLINE MEDIA ADVERTISING ESSENTIALLY IMPLIES THE UTILIZATION OF DIFFERENT SITES, ESPECIALLY FRIENDLY ORGANIZING DESTINATIONS, TO DRIVE MORE TRAFFIC TO YOUR OWN SITE. SUCH SITES WOULD BE THE PREFERENCES OF YOUTUBE, FACEBOOK, LINKEDIN, MYSPACE,

AMONG OTHERS. SINCE THESE SITES ARE BEING UTILIZED BY THOUSANDS, IN THE EVENT THAT NOT LARGE NUMBER OF CLIENTS AROUND THE WORLD, THEY ARE INCREDIBLE TO EXPLOIT TO

DRIVE MORE TRAFFIC TO YOUR SITE. DIRECTING PEOPLE TO YOUR SITE IS REALLY ONE OF THE MOST SIGNIFICANT

THINGS THAT YOU WANT TO ACCOMPLISH, TO ACQUIRE BENEFITS FROM THE ITEMS OR ADMINISTRATIONS THAT

YOU OFFER THROUGH IT. WITH MORE INDIVIDUALS VISITING YOUR SITE, YOU WILL HAVE MORE CHANCES OF UNCOVERING YOUR ITEMS, AND INCREMENT THE ODDS OF ACQUIRING BENEFITS FROM IT. REMEMBER THAT THERE ARE SURE ADVANCES THAT YOU REALLY WANT TO TAKE TO EXPLOIT SUCH SITES. BESIDE SETTING UP A RECORD APPROPRIATELY IN EVERY ONE OF THE SITES YOU WILL MAKE

UTILIZATION OF, YOU ADDITIONALLY NEED TO CONCOCT COURSES TO HAVE MORE INDIVIDUALS FOLLOW YOUR POSTS, AND THE CONNECTIONS THAT YOU WOULD PUT FOR YOU, WHICH LEAD TO THE PRINCIPLE SITE THAT YOU ARE

LEADING YOUR ONLINE BUSINESS ON.

THE SECOND SORT OF ONLINE MEDIA ADVERTISING AS REFERENCED ON TOP IS WEBPAGE LOCATION. IN SPITE OF THE FACT THAT YOU WOULD BE ABLE

AS OF NOW POTENTIALLY
ACQUIRE VOLUME OF
TRAFFIC THROUGH YOUR
OFF-SITE WEB-BASED
MEDIA SHOWCASING
ENDEAVORS,
YOU WANT TO UTILIZE
NEARBY ARRANGEMENTS,
TO ENSURE THAT
INDIVIDUALS STAY
SUFFICIENTLY LONG
IN YOUR OWN SITE TO
LOOK AT WHAT YOU BRING
TO THE TABLE TO THEM.
THIS WOULD IMPLY THAT
YOU
NEED TO FURTHER
DEVELOP THE SORT OF
CONTENT THAT YOU HAVE

FOR YOUR SITE, UTILIZE SPECIFIC PROCEDURES TO ACQUIRE YOUR OWN IMAGE CHARACTER, DRIVE NATURAL TRAFFIC FROM WEB CRAWLER, AND SUCH. BASICALLY, THESE TWO KINDS OF ONLINE MEDIA ADVERTISING WORK CONNECTED AT THE HIP IN ACQUIRING YOU MORE BENEFITS IN YOUR BUSINESS. HENCE, IT IS BEST THAT YOU UTILIZE THEM BOTH, SO YOU WILL BE CAPABLE TO ACCOMPLISH THE ACHIEVEMENT THAT YOU HAVE BEEN YEARNING FOR.

HOW MIGHT SOCIAL MEDIA BENEFIT YOUR BUSINESS.

WEB-BASED MEDIA SHOWCASING IS ONE OF THE TOP MOST WEB BASED ADVERTISING TECHNIQUES THAT WEB ADVERTISERS, AND SURPRISINGLY NEIGHBORHOOD ORGANIZATIONS UTILIZE TODAY. THIS IS ON THE GROUNDS THAT WEB-BASED MEDIA SITES ARE BEING PARTAKEN BY A GREAT MANY INDIVIDUALS AROUND THE WORLD TODAY.

ARE REGULARLY VISITING THESE PERSON TO PERSON COMMUNICATION DESTINATIONS ON A ORDINARY PREMISE, AND ON THE OFF CHANCE THAT YOU CAN REACH OUT TO THE GREATER PART OF THEM, YOU WILL HAVE THE

SHOT AT HELPING YOUR BENEFITS TO AN EXTREMELY SIGNIFICANT LEVEL.
ASSUMING YOU CAN DO YOUR BEST,

ONE OF THE ADVANTAGES
THAT YOUR ONLINE
BUSINESS CAN DETERMINE
FROM WEB-BASED MEDIA
IS OPENNESS. AT THE END
OF THE DAY, ASSUMING
YOU ARE WORKING YOUR
ONLINE BUSINESS
THROUGH
YOUR OWN SITE, YOU CAN
EXPLOIT ONLINE MEDIA
SHOWCASING TO ACQUIRE
COLOSSAL
VOLUMES OF TRAFFIC
TOWARDS IT. THE MORE
VOLUME OF DESIGNATED
SITE TRAFFIC YOU CAN
GET FROM

SITES LIKE YOUTUBE, FACEBOOK, MYSPACE, AND SUCH, THE MORE POTENTIAL YOU HAVE IN EXPANDING THE QUANTITY OF DEALS FOR THE ITEMS THAT YOU HAVE ON YOUR PAGE. YOU WANT TO REMEMBER HOWEVER THAT THE VAST MAJORITY WHO REGISTER TO THESE INFORMAL COMMUNICATION DESTINATIONS ARE THE PEOPLE WHO NEED TO REACH OUT AND FIND THEIR

ONES. BESIDE THAT, SOME LIKEWISE REGISTER WITH THE DESIRE FOR MEETING THAT UNIQUE INDIVIDUAL WHO HAS BEEN SLIPPERY ALL THESE YEARS. ALONG THESE LINES, BEFORE YOU ACQUAINT YOUR BUSINESS WITH THEM, YOU SHOULD ASSEMBLE CONNECTIONS FIRST, TO ACQUIRE THEIR TRUST. BESIDE THAT, YOU OUGHT TO LIKEWISE ASSEMBLE YOUR BY ENGAGING WITH SPECIFIC CONVERSATIONS AND OFFER SIGNIFICANT

PERSPECTIVES ABOUT IT, OR BY SHARING SPECIFIC SUBSTANCE FOUND ON YOUR SITE, WHICH MIGHT BE USEFUL TO INDIVIDUALS WHO HAVE A PLACE WITH TARGET MARKET. BY DOING THAT, INDIVIDUALS YOU CONTINUALLY REACH OUT TO THROUGH THESE SOCIAL MEDIA STAGES WILL BEFORE LONG EXPECT MORE FROM YOU; AND THAT IS THE LEGITIMATE TIME THAT YOU ACQUAINT YOUR BUSINESS WITH THEM.

BESIDE DRIVING MORE
TRAFFIC TO YOUR
WEBPAGE, WHEN YOU
HAVE SET UP YOUR
ONLINE BUSINESS TO
YOUR
PEERS ON THESE LONG
RANGE INTERPERSONAL
COMMUNICATION
LOCALES, ANOTHER
ADVANTAGE YOU CAN GET
FROM IT IS TO GET
FAIR INPUT WITH
REGARDS TO THE ITEMS
OR ADMINISTRATIONS
THAT YOU ARE
PRESENTLY ADVERTISING.
THUSLY,

YOU
WILL ACTUALLY WANT TO
GADGET CERTAIN
TECHNIQUES OR
ADJUSTMENTS, TO
FURTHER DEVELOP YOUR
BUSINESS.
SINCE THE INPUTS YOU
ARE GETTING ARE GIVEN
BY INDIVIDUALS WHO
HAVE A PLACE WITH YOUR
OBJECTIVE MARKET,
YOU WILL ACTUALLY
WANT TO DECIDE THE
LEGITIMATE STRIDES TO
ACQUIRE ACHIEVEMENT
IN YOUR BUSINESS.
THESE ARE ONLY A
PORTION OF THE

ADVANTAGES YOUR BUSINESS CAN GET FROM ONLINE MEDIA. REMEMBER THAT BY ENGAGING WITH THESE INFORMAL COMMUNICATION DESTINATIONS, IT WILL LIKEWISE ASSIST YOU WITH DISTINGUISHING THE NECESSITIES OF INDIVIDUALS INSIDE YOUR OBJECTIVE MARKET. HENCE, IT WILL LIKEWISE HELP YOU NOT SIMPLY IN ADJUSTING YOUR CURRENT ITEM, YET IN ADDITION PERHAPS FOSTER

ANOTHER ITEM, WHICH
INDIVIDUALS WILL TRULY
APPRECIATE AND
SUPPORT.
END
ALL IN ALL, YOU SHOULD
NOW HAVE A MORE CLEAR
IMAGE OF WHAT ONLINE
MEDIA IS, WHAT IT CAN
DO, AND
HOW IT CAN HELP YOU. AS
REFERENCED ABOVE,
THERE ARE VARIOUS
WAYS THAT YOU CAN
UTILIZE WEB-BASED
MEDIA TO ADVANCE YOUR
SITE. BY RECALLING THE
PREVIOUSLY MENTIONED
FOCUSES AND

TIPS, YOU CAN PROFIT FROM UTILIZING WEB-BASED MEDIA TO ADVANCE YOUR SITE. HENCE, BEGIN LOOKING FOR WEB-BASED MEDIA LOCALES YOU CAN USE TO ADVANCE YOUR SITE OR ON THE WEB BUSINESS TODAY AND BEGIN UTILIZING THEM. BEFORE LONG, YOU WILL ACTUALLY WANT TO SEE AN EXPANSION IN THE QUANTITY OF GUESTS TO YOUR SITE AND INFER ADVANTAGES, FOR EXAMPLE, MORE DEALS AND CASH FROM THIS ADDITIONAL

WHEN THE NEW HIGHLIGHTS VIA WEB-BASED MEDIA STAGES GET DECLARED, SOCIAL MEDIA ADVERTISERS REGULARLY ATTEMPT TO DECIDE THE EXPENSE AND THE ADVANTAGES OF UTILIZING

SPECIFIC ELEMENTS FOR THEIR BUSINESS. THEY NEED TO CHOOSE WHETHER THE EXPENSE OF

FIGURING OUT HOW TO UTILIZE ANOTHER COMPONENT WILL BE WORTH THE EFFORT,

AND WHETHER OR NOT IT WOULD CONVERT INTO ADDITIONAL COMMITMENT AND DEALS.

THE INSTAGRAM GUIDES HIGHLIGHT IS A BETTER APPROACH TO SHARE DATA AND PROPOSALS WITH YOUR DEVOTEES. VIABLY, WHILE MAKING A GUIDE, YOU ARE MAKING A BLOG ENTRY THAT IS CONTAINED OTHER INSTAGRAM POSTS HOWEVER IS CONSTRUCTED INTO THE INSTAGRAM STAGE.

DEVELOPMENT CAN APPEAR TO BE UNIQUE FOR VARIOUS ORGANIZATIONS. THE OBJECTIVES OF DEVELOPMENT RELY UPON THE POINTS OF THE BRAND AND THE REASON FOR THE SUBSTANCE PROCEDURE IS.

WHEN ATTEMPTING TO DEVELOP YOUR IMAGE, IT IS VITAL TO PUT FORTH UNMISTAKABLE OBJECTIVES. THIS WILL GUARANTEE THAT YOU ARE ON TARGET AND POSTING VIABLY. IT

ADEQUATELY ISN'T TO JUST
POST; YOU SHOULD POST
ADEQUATELY.
DEVELOPMENT ON
INSTAGRAM CAN LOOK
LIKE NUMEROUS THINGS.
ONE OF THE MOST WIDELY
RECOGNIZED
DEVELOPMENT
MEASUREMENTS IS
SUPPORTER
DEVELOPMENT. ALONG
THESE LINES,
MAYBE YOU NEED TO
EXPAND YOUR
GENERALLY SPEAKING
ADHERENT COUNT.

WHILE DOING THIS, YOU REALLY WANT TO RECALL THE DISTINCTION BETWEEN THE QUANTITY OF ADHERENTS, AND DREW IN SUPPORTERS. THIS MEANS GUARANTEEING THAT YOUR DEVOTEES REALLY CARE ABOUT YOUR BUSINESS AND ASSOCIATE WITH YOUR SUBSTANCE UTILIZES GUIDES ADEQUATELY IS AN EXTRAORDINARY METHOD FOR FOCUSING ON INTRIGUED CLIENTS.

DEVELOPMENT WITH INSTAGRAM GUIDES IS LIKE DEVELOPMENT IN DIFFERENT REGIONS AND POST
TYPES. THE STANDARDS AND FUNDAMENTAL HYPOTHETICAL UNDERSTANDINGS OF DEVELOPMENT ARE THE EXACTLY.THERE ARE THREE SORTS OF INSTAGRAM GUIDES: SPOTS, ITEMS, AND POSTS.
1: SET THE PRINCIPLES AND STICK OUT NORMALLY, AS INSTAGRAM GUIDES ARE ANOTHER COMPONENT

THERE ARE NO SHOWS OR
ANTICIPATED POSTS. THIS
IMPLIES THAT YOU GET TO
MAKE THE STANDARDS.
ONCE YOUR
CROWD HAS AN
ASSUMPTION FOR A SORT
OF POST THE PRINCIPLES
INCREMENT
DRAMATICALLY. FOR THIS
REASON THERE ARE SUCH
COUNTLESS COMPONENTS
OF POSTS THAT ARE
RELIABLY DUPLICATED
ACROSS MANY RECORDS;
 SINCE THOSE ARE THE
THINGS

THAT WORK. AT THE POINT WHEN CLIENTS VIEW A FEED POST, SPECIFICALLY A BRAND POST, THEY HAVE CERTAIN ASSUMPTIONS THAT SHOULD BE MET, OR THEY WILL WITHDRAW. BE THAT AS IT MAY, WITH GUIDES, NOTWITHSTANDING, YOU CAN BE A PIECE OF THE PROGRESSIVE CLIENTS WHO GET TO CHOOSE THE STANDARDS. THERE IS NO SUCH THING AS SHOWS

AND EXPECTED
ORGANIZATIONS AS OF
HOWEVER IMPLYING THAT
YOU CAN BE JUST ABOUT
AS IMAGINATIVE AND
ENERGIZING AS YOU NEED.
IT IS LIKEWISE ESSENTIAL
TO TAKE NOTE OF THAT
CROWDS MAY NOT BE
RESPONSIVE TO
UNDERTAKING NEW
HIGHLIGHTS AND TYPES
OF POSTS. THIS IMPLIES
YOU GET TO TEMPT
THEM. YOU BECAME THE
SECTION INTO THE
UNIVERSE OF

INSTAGRAM GUIDES FOR
THEM.
ALL THINGS CONSIDERED,
BEING ONE OF THE
PRIMARY INDIVIDUALS TO
UTILIZE ANOTHER
COMPONENT, AND USE IT
ALL THINGS CONSIDERED,
IS INTEGRAL TO A
DEVELOPING CROWD. IT
WILL SHOW THAT YOU ARE
ON-PATTERN AND
APPLICABLE -
CONSIDERING HOW QUICK
WE ARE ACCUSTOMED TO
GETTING DATA AND HOW
ACCLIMATED WE ARE TO
MOMENT DELIGHT WE
JUST NEED TO

GET DO
YOU TRACK DOWN
PERTINENT DATA.2:
PROMOTING YOUR
SUBSTANCE
HAVING THE OPTION TO
ADVANCE YOUR
SUBSTANCE IS THE MOST
EFFECTIVE WAY TO
DEVELOP YOUR CROWD.
ADVANCEMENT RUNS TWO
DIFFERENT WAYS; FIRST
ADVANCING YOUR
SUBSTANCE THROUGH
INSTAGRAM
GUIDES, AND SECOND,
ADVANCING YOUR GUIDE.
UTILIZING THE ITEM
GUIDE, YOU WILL

ACTUALLY WANT TO
MAKE BITS OF
KNOWLEDGE INTO THE
ITEM
THAT YOU ARE SELLING
ON INSTAGRAM.
FREQUENTLY
INDIVIDUALS WOULD LIKE
TO FIND OUT ABOUT
AN ITEM PRIOR TO
FOCUSING ON
PURCHASING, SEE MAKING
A GUIDE TO YOUR ITEMS
IS AN EXTRAORDINARY
METHOD FOR SHOWING
YOUR CROWD MORE. IT
VERY WELL MAY BE THE
DISTINCTION

BETWEEN A DEAL AND NOT. ANYTHING YOU DO TO ASSIST WITH MAKING YOUR ITEMS IS GREAT ALSO WILL ASSIST YOU WITH DEVELOPING YOUR CROWD. IT WILL LIKEWISE AID THE DEVELOPMENT OF YOUR

BUSINESS, AND MAKING AN INTERPRETATION OF PERSPECTIVES INTO DEALS.

ASSUMING YOUR BUSINESS HAS AN ACTUAL AREA UTILIZING THE SPOT GUIDE IS AN EXTRAORDINARY WAY

TO SHOW IT OFF. YOU CAN
MAKE A GUIDE INTO A
WIDE RANGE OF
COMPONENTS OF YOUR
BUSINESS; IT VERY WELL
MAY BE A COMPELLING
APPROACH TO IMPARTING
TO YOUR CROWD WHAT
YOUR IMAGE IS ABOUT.
YOU CAN SHARE
INSTRUCTIVE SUBSTANCE
ABOUT COMPONENTS OF
YOUR BUSINESS, AND
MAKE A SIMPLE WAY FOR
YOUR CROWD TO SHARE
YOUR IMAGE
WITH THEIR LOVED ONES.

BY REMEMBERING YOUR
POST FOR THE "POSTS"
GUIDE, YOU ARE VIABLY
ADVANCING THAT
CONTENT, AS WELL.
REGARDLESS OF WHETHER
YOUR GUIDES ARE
INCLUDED TOTALLY OF
YOUR OWN POSTS,
OR THEN AGAIN YOU ARE
MAKING AN
ARRANGEMENT OF MANY
CLIENT'S POSTS; HAVING
YOUR OWN POST
IN THERE IS AN
ADVANCEMENT OF YOUR
SUBSTANCE.
 THE EQUIVALENT GOES
FOR IN THE EVENT

THAT YOUR POST IS
REMEMBERED FOR ONE
MORE CLIENT'S GUIDE-IT
IS A SIMPLE
ADVANCEMENT OF YOUR
SUBSTANCE.
THESE THREE SORTS OF
GUIDES; ITEMS, PLACES,
AND POSTS, ALL HAVE
UNIQUE,
HOWEVER SUCCESSFUL
RAMIFICATIONS FOR
DEVELOPING YOUR CROWD
AND BUSINESS.
WITH RESPECT TO THE
ADVANCEMENT OF THE
INSTAGRAM GUIDE ITSELF,
THERE ARE A FEW ROADS
YOU CAN TAKE.

BASICALLY, HOWEVER, YOU WILL DEPEND ON SHARES. YOU SHOULD SHARE YOUR POSTS TO YOUR STORY AND FURTHERMORE URGE YOUR CROWD TO DO LIKEWISE. AT LAST, INSTAGRAM GUIDES WILL APPEAR ON THE INVESTIGATE PAGE, YET UP TO THAT POINT YOU WANT TO ADVANCE THEM NATURALLY. ADVANCING YOUR OVERALL SUBSTANCE, AS WELL, WILL LIKEWISE IN THIS MANNER ADVANCE YOUR

GUIDES. UTILIZING HASHTAGS ADD AREA GEOTAGS ON YOUR STANDARD FEED POST IS A PHENOMENAL METHOD FOR DOING THIS. PASS ON A REFERENCE IN YOUR INSCRIPTION TO YOUR GUIDE TO DIRECT YOUR CROWD OVER TO YOUR PROFILE AND ONTO THE GUIDE. FOR INSTANCE, CARRYING OUT SUPPORTED POSTS IS AN INCREDIBLE METHOD FOR COMING TO NEW

CROWD INDIVIDUALS. INSTAGRAM ADVERTISEMENTS WILL BE ESPECIALLY VALUABLE ON THE OFF CHANCE THAT YOU EITHER HAVE A SHOP ON INSTAGRAM OR A BUSINESS WITH AN ACTUAL AREA. GENERALLY, YOU SHOULD HAVE THE OPTION TO ADVANCE YOUR SUBSTANCE AND THAT IMPLIES ALL SORTS OF YOUR SUBSTANCE. GETTING INDIVIDUALS TO YOUR PROFILE OUGHT TO BE THE

INITIAL STEP,
AND AFTERWARD HAVING
SUCH EXCELLENT
SUBSTANCE THAT YOUR
CROWD CAN'T HELP IT
HITTING THE FOLLOW
BUTTON. IT OUGHT TO BE
SIMPLE AND CLEAR ON
YOUR PROFILE TO SEE
PRECISELY WHAT'S
REALLY GOING ON WITH
YOUR BUSINESS, WHICH
DRIVES US INTO 3: EXPERT
MARKING
MAKING INSTAGRAM
GUIDES IS AN INCREDIBLE
METHOD FOR
FACILITATING YOUR
MARKING WHICH WILL

ASSIST YOU WITH DEVELOPING YOUR BUSINESS. MARKING IS CRUCIAL FOR DEVELOPMENT. ADEQUATELY, MARKING IS THE INSIGHT THAT YOUR CROWD HAS OF YOUR BUSINESS. YOUR IMAGE NEEDS TO THINK ABOUT THE REQUIREMENTS AND NEEDS OF YOUR OBJECTIVE CROWD AND IT SHOULD BE PROPER FOR YOUR SUBSTANCE. MARKING PROCEDURES NORMALLY INCLUDE RAISING BRAND

MINDFULNESS,
ACQUIRING
MEMORABILITY, AND,
AT LAST, ACCOMPLISHING
BRAND RELIABILITY.
INSTAGRAM GUIDES WILL
ADD ANOTHER ASPECT TO
YOUR IMAGE.
INSTAGRAM GUIDES ARE A
METHOD FOR
SHOWCASING YOURSELF
AS A SPECIALIST; ONE OF
THE
CRUCIAL MAINSTAYS OF
PROMOTING AND
MARKING. YOUR CROWD
NEEDS TO TRUST
YOU AND THEY NEED TO
ACCEPT THAT YOU ARE

DEPENDABLE WELLSPRING OF DATA. CONSIDERING ALL THE TRICK AND SPAM ACCOUNTS THAT ARE OUT THERE, YOU WANT TO DO ANYTHING YOU CAN TO GUARANTEE THAT YOUR CROWD ACCEPTS THAT YOU ARE GENUINE AND SIGNIFICANT.
YOU OUGHT TO LIKEWISE GUARANTEE THAT YOUR RECORD IS SET UP AS A BUSINESS PROFILE. THIS ADDS A DEGREE OF IMPRESSIVE SKILL. IN WEB-BASED MEDIA, APPEARANCES MEAN THE

SO YOU SHOULD MAKE A
MOVE TO GRANDSTAND
YOUR IMAGE.
THIS WILL ASSIST YOU
WITH DEVELOPING IN
LIGHT OF THE FACT THAT
MAIN BRANDS SUCCEED.
IRREGULAR BUSINESS
ACCOUNTS LOSE ALL
SENSE OF DIRECTION IN
THE MESSINESS AND
OVERLOOKED. MARKING IS
ESSENTIAL TO
DEVELOPMENT; IT ASSISTS
WITH CLEARNESS AND
AMAZING SKILL.

4: DEPTH TO YOUR POSTS

INSTAGRAM GUIDES ARE AN INCREDIBLE METHOD FOR ADDING A DEGREE OF PROFUNDITY TO YOUR POSTS. YOU CAN DEVELOP YOUR SUBSTANCE AND ADD MORE DETAIL TO SUBJECTS THAT YOU HAVE EFFECTIVELY SHARED ON YOUR FEED. GATHERING YOUR POSTS BY SUBJECT OR TOPIC IN A GUIDE IS AN INCREDIBLE MANNER TO COORDINATE

YOUR CROWD TO A SPECIFIC COMPONENT OF YOUR APTITUDE. BUILDING GUIDES AROUND SPECIFIC THOUGHTS AND IDEAS IS AN INCREDIBLE METHOD FOR SHOWING YOUR CROWD WHAT YOU CAN OFFER THEM, PAST STRAIGHTFORWARD FEED CONTENT. THIS WILL ASSIST YOU WITH DEVELOPING SINCE CROWDS DON'T NEED SURFACE-LEVEL SUBSTANCE.

THEY NEED TO KNOW WHO THEY ARE SUPPORTING, AND THEY NEED TO FEEL LIKE THEY
ARE A PIECE OF IT. THERE ARE HUGE NUMBER OF BRANDS THAT CLIENTS ARE PRESENTED TO ON A DAY BY DAY LEVEL, YET THEY NEED TO FABRICATE AN ASSOCIATION, ALL THINGS BEING EQUAL.
THE EXPLANATION THAT INSTAGRAM EXECUTED GUIDES WAS TO MAKE IT MORE STRAIGHTFORWARD FOR
CLIENTS TO GIVE AND GET PROPOSALS, TIPS,

GIVES YOU
THE POTENTIAL CHANCE
TO MAKE A MORE
PROFOUND ASSOCIATION
WITH YOUR CROWD. TO BE
CAPABLE
TO SHARE EXTRA DATA,
REGARDLESS OF WHETHER
IT BE ABOUT ITEMS,
PLACES, OR POSTS,
IS A PHENOMENAL
METHOD FOR FURTHER
DEVELOPING YOUR
MARKING.
INDEPENDENT OF
WHETHER YOU DECIDE TO
ENHANCE YOUR OWN
POSTS WITH POSTS
FROM DIFFERENT CLIENTS

YOU CAN EVEN MORE
YOUR MARKING
OBJECTIVES. HOWEVER,
ON THE OFF CHANCE THAT
YOU DECIDE TO
INCORPORATE OTHER
CLIENT'S POSTS IN WITH
YOUR OWN SUBSTANCE,
YOU ARE
LIKEWISE INCORPORATING
YOUR OWN SUBSTANCE IN
THE DISCUSSION.
DIFFERENT CLIENTS WILL
PROBABLY
SHARE YOUR POSTS,
CONSEQUENTLY
PRESENTING YOUR
SUBSTANCE TO NEW
CROWDS. IN ANY CASE,

BY
BEING SPECIFIC WITH
REGARDS TO THE
SUBSTANCE THAT YOU
SHARE, AND JUST
INCLUDING CONTENT
FROM RESPECTABLE
BRANDS WITH AN AFTER
THAT IS LIKE YOUR IDEAL
INTEREST GROUP,
YOU WILL ADD
PROFUNDITY TO YOUR
SUBSTANCE AND DEVELOP
YOUR BUSINESS.
5: COLLABORATION
INSTAGRAM GUIDES ARE
ADDITIONALLY AN
INCREDIBLE METHOD FOR
TEAMING UP WITH NEW
AND UNIQUE

ACCOUNTS. AS YOU CAN ADD POSTS FROM ANY CLIENT INTO YOUR GUIDES IT IS A EXTRAORDINARY METHOD FOR GROWING YOUR ORGANIZATION OF ASSOCIATIONS. COOPERATION IS PROBABLY THE MOST AMAZING ASPECT OF INSTAGRAM. HAVING THE OPTION TO MAKE CONTENT WITH ANOTHER CLIENT IS A PHENOMENAL METHOD FOR REINFORCING BOTH OF YOUR BRANDS. MAKING GUIDES FOR

VARIOUS TYPES OF
ORGANIZATIONS, FOR
INSTANCE; BISTROS,
USED STORES TOP OF THE
LINE STORES,
INDEPENDENT VENTURES,
BASEMENT ENTRYWAYS,
PIZZA
CAFÉS, WHATEVER IT
VERY WELL MIGHT BE MAY
PROMPT SPONSORSHIP
AMAZING OPEN DOORS AS
WELL.
ORGANIZATIONS NEED TO
ADVANCE THEMSELVES
THROUGH IMPACTS AND
BRANDS THAT
THEY TRUST

AND ARE TRUSTED BY
THEIR CROWD. IN THIS
MANNER, IN THE EVENT
THAT YOU HAVE UTILIZED
DIRECTS SUCCESSFULLY
PREVIOUSLY AND
INTRODUCED YOURSELF
AS A POWER AND A
TRAILBLAZER IT IS
CONCEIVABLE THAT
BRANDS WILL NEED TO
TEAM UP WITH YOU ALL
TOGETHER
TO DEVELOP THEIR CROWD
WHICH WILL, THUS,
DEVELOP YOURS.
CLIENTS LIKEWISE LOVE
TO SEE JOINT EFFORTS.

THEY REGULARLY TRUST
THE BRANDS THAT THEIR
MOST LOVED BRANDS
POST ABOUT. TRACKING
DOWN SPECIAL AND
ENERGIZING OPEN DOORS
TO
TEAM UP WITH IS AN
EXTRAORDINARY METHOD
FOR DEVELOPING YOUR
CROWD. GUIDES ARE AN
AWESOME,
WHAT'S MORE SIMPLE
METHOD FOR WORKING
TOGETHER WITH NEW
CLIENTS.
MOREOVER, WHENEVER
YOU HAVE CONSTRUCTED
A SOLID STANDING,

AND COORDINATED YOUR CONTENT INTO THE MORE EXTENSIVE LOCAL AREA, YOUR POSTS MIGHT BE REMEMBERED FOR OTHER GUIDES TOO. THIS WILL ASSIST WITH PRESENTING YOUR RECORD TO NEW INDIVIDUALS, WHICH WILL CONVERT INTO NEW SUPPORTERS AND IN GENERAL BRAND DEVELOPMENT.

BY AND LARGE, INSTAGRAM GUIDES BRING NUMEROUS NEW OPEN DOORS FOR DEVELOPMENT.

CONCLUSION

INSTAGRAM GUIDES ARE AN AWESOME METHOD FOR ASSISTING YOU WITH DEVELOPING YOUR CROWD.
HOWEVER, YOU SHOULD DON'T DISREGARD THE ATTEMPTED AND TRIED STRATEGIES
YOU HAVE FOR DEVELOPMENT. ON THE OFF CHANCE THAT YOU HAVE FOUND ACHIEVEMENT IN ONE REGION PROCEED TO DO AS SUCH. NONETHELESS,

NEW UNDERTAKINGS CAN
SUPPLEMENT YOUR
CURRENT SYSTEMS AT
THE SAME TIME,
IN SOME MEASURE AT
FIRST, OUGHT NOT
DOMINATE THEM.
BASICALLY, THE MAIN
WAY YOU
WILL KNOW WHETHER
SOMETHING WILL BE
FRUITFUL IS TO ATTEMPT.
YOU SHOULD SCREEN AND
CHECKING YOUR
INVESTIGATION AND SEE
WHICH
TECHNIQUES ARE
FURNISHING YOU WITH

THE OUTCOMES THAT ARE
IN ACCORDANCE WITH
YOUR BUSINESS
OBJECTIVES. REALLY
TAKE A LOOK AT YOUR
COMMITMENT,
INVESTIGATION, AND BITS
OF KNOWLEDGE;
UTILIZING WORKED IN
APPARATUSES, AS
WELL AS OUTSIDER
APPARATUSES, AND
GAUGE AND EVALUATE
THE THINGS THAT YOU
ARE
DOING AND HOW THEY
ARE GIVING YOU THE
OUTCOMES THAT YOU
NEED FOR YOUR IMAGE.

INSTAGRAM GUIDES ARE
AN ESPECIALLY
INTRIGUING COMPONENT
THAT YOU CAN USE TO
DEVELOP
YOUR IMAGE. MAKE THE
MOST OF THE CHANCE TO
INTRODUCE YOURSELF
AND A
CONFIDED IN WELLSPRING
OF DATA, JUST AS AN
ESTEEMED ASSET IN YOUR
INDUSTRY,
ALSO WATCH YOUR IMAGE
DEVELOP!

BASIC

DO YOU HAVE A PLACE WITH A WEB-BASED INFORMAL COMMUNICATION SITE? WITH THEIR NEW ASCENT IN PROMINENCE THERE IS A DECENT POSSIBILITY THAT YOU DO.
BE THAT AS IT MAY, IT IS SOMETHING TO BE A LOCAL AREA PART AND ONE MORE TO DEFINITELY TAKE PART IN INTERNET BASED CONVERSATIONS, JUST AS THE NUMEROUS OTHER ORGANIZATION HIGHLIGHTS.

NUMEROUS WEB CLIENTS AS OF NOW IMAGINE THAT THEY KNOW ALL THAT THEY NEED TO BE AWARE OF THEIR INTERPERSONAL INTERACTION LOCAL AREA. TRAGICALLY, NOT EVERY PERSON DOES. TRUTH BE TOLD, YOU CAN FIND VARIOUS POSTS ONLINE OF INDIVIDUALS BLUSTERING OR EXPRESSING THAT THEY WANTED THAT THEIR INTERPERSONAL INTERACTION SITE, LIKE YAHOO! 360, MYSPACE, ORKUT, FRIENDWISE, OR

FRIENDFINDER, HAS A
SPECIFIC ASSISTANCE AND
ELEMENT. TOO OFTEN,
THOSE BANNERS DIDN'T
LOOK BEFORE THEY
BEGAN TALKING ON THE
GROUNDS THAT,
INCIDENTALLY,
NUMEROUS
INTERPERSONAL
INTERACTION SITES HAVE
WHAT INDIVIDUALS NEED,
JUST EVERYBODY DOESN'T
BE AWARE OF IT.
THE INITIAL PHASE, IN
MAKING THE MOST OUT OF
YOUR LONG

RANGE INFORMAL
COMMUNICATION
EXPERIENCE, IS TO
ACCLIMATE YOURSELF TO
THE INTERNET BASED
LOCAL AREA OR
NETWORKS THAT YOU
HAVE A PLACE WITH. THIS
SHOULD EFFORTLESSLY BE
POSSIBLE BY INTENTLY
INSPECTING THE SITE.
THERE ARE SUCH A LARGE
NUMBER OF WEB CLIENTS
WHO ARE CENTERED
AROUND MEETING NEW
COMPANIONS THAT THEY
MOVE BEGAN
IMMEDIATELY.

WHILE IT IS GREAT TO
BEGIN MEETING NEW
INDIVIDUALS
IMMEDIATELY, IT IS
LIKEWISE GREAT TO
KNOW WHAT YOUR LONG
RANGE INFORMAL
COMMUNICATION SITE
BRINGS TO THE TABLE.
THIS MUST BE FINISHED
BY INTENTLY LOOKING AT
THE SITE. REGARDLESS OF
WHETHER YOU REQUIRE
ONE HOUR OR ONE DAY
LOOKING AT THE SITE,
YOU WILL PROBABLY BE
SATISFIED WITH YOUR
CHOICE TO MAKE IT
HAPPEN.

WHILE LOOKING AT THE SITE OF THE WEB-BASED LOCAL AREA THAT YOU HAVE A PLACE WITH, IT IS EDUCATED THAT YOU INSPECT THE TERMS REGARDING USE UNDERSTANDING. THIS UNDERSTANDING REGULARLY TRACES WHAT YOU SHOULD OR SHOULDN'T DO ON THE WEB. REGARDLESS OF THE WAY THAT COUNTLESS WEB BASED SYSTEMS ADMINISTRATION LOCALES, LIKE MYSPACE, HAVE LITTLE GUIDELINES, THERE ARE DIFFERENT

WEB-BASED MEDIA MARKETING SCENE THESE PRINCIPLES AND LIMITATIONS MIGHT RESTRICT THE SUBSTANCE THAT YOU CAN HAVE ON YOUR SITE, JUST AS YOUR PHOTOS, RECORDINGS, AND DIFFERENT MEDIA. NUMEROUS SITES, INCLUDING PERSON TO PERSON COMMUNICATION SITES, WILL END YOUR PARTICIPATION ASSUMING YOU ARE FOUND ABUSING THESE ARRANGEMENTS. BY PERUSING THE GUIDELINES AS A WHOLE AND LIMITATIONS

OF THE INTERPERSONAL
INTERACTION SITE YOU
HAVE A PLACE WITH, YOU
OUGHT TO HAVE THE
OPTION TO GUARANTEE
THAT YOU CAN PROCEED
TO UTILIZE AND PARTAKE
IN THE SITE.
ONE OF THE MANY
ADVANTAGES TO
COMPLETELY INSPECTING
THE INTERPERSONAL
ORGANIZATION YOU HAVE
A PLACE WITH IS THAT
YOU COULD BE MADE
AWARE OF ORGANIZATION
ADVANTAGES,
ELEMENTS, OR
ADMINISTRATIONS

THAT YOU WERE
ALREADY UNINFORMED
ABOUT.
AS WELL AS GIVING YOU
YOUR OWN PROFILE PAGE
AND PERMITTING YOU TO
WELCOME OTHER WEB
CLIENTS INTO YOUR
ORGANIZATION, THERE
ARE VARIOUS DIFFERENT
THINGS THAT YOU CAN DO
WITH ONLINE LONG
RANGE INTERPERSONAL
COMMUNICATION SITES.
AN ENORMOUS NUMBER OF
SITES HAVE MADE
ELEMENTS AND SEGMENTS
THAT INCORPORATE
HOROSCOPES, TESTS,

SURVEYS, TEXTING, VISIT ROOMS, AND SUBSTANTIALLY MORE. IN ANY CASE, BEFORE YOU UTILIZE THESE PART BENEFITS, YOU SHOULD REALIZE THAT THEY EXIST.

ASSUMING YOU ARE KEEN ON MAKING NEW INTERNET BASED COMPANIONS, ALMOST CERTAINLY, YOU HAVE AS OF NOW JOINED A WEB-BASED INFORMAL COMMUNICATION LOCAL AREA. REGARDLESS OF WHETHER YOU ARE KEEN ON JOINING MORE OR YOU

ARE A FIRST-TIME CLIENT, YOU WILL TO PAINSTAKINGLY PICK YOUR ORGANIZATIONS. BY INVESTIGATING EVERY LONG RANGE INTERPERSONAL COMMUNICATION SITE ON THE WEB, YOU OUGHT TO EFFORTLESSLY HAVE THE OPTION TO FINISH YOURSELF WITH THE BENEFITS AND INCONVENIENCES OF EACH. WHAT'S MORE, SINCE MOST PERSON TO PERSON COMMUNICATION SITES ARE ALLOWED TO USE, THERE ARE NO DANGERS

RELATED WITH CHECKING THE ORGANIZATION OUT. ASSUMING YOU END UP GOING OVER A SITE THAT REQUIRES A PAID PARTICIPATION AND YOU MIGHT WANT TO ATTEMPT IT, YOU ARE ENCOURAGED TO POST WITH THE EXPECTATION OF COMPLIMENTARY ENROLLMENT PLANS OR FREE PATH PERIODS. THEY MIGHT HAVE THE OPTION TO ASSIST YOU WITH DECIDING IF THE INTERPERSONAL INTERACTION SITE THAT YOU ARE KEEN

JOINING MERITS THE
EXPENSE.
AS MAY BE OBVIOUS,
THERE ARE VARIOUS
APPROACHES TO MAKING
THE MOST OUT OF YOUR
PERSON TO PERSON
COMMUNICATION
EXPERIENCE. THE
CONTROL IS IN YOUR
GRASP. IT IS YOUR CHOICE
CONCERNING WHETHER
OR NOT YOU NEED TO
INVEST A LIMITED
QUANTITY OF ENERGY
INVESTIGATING YOUR
ORGANIZATION AND ALL
THAT IT BRINGS TO THE
TABLE.

NOTWITHSTANDING, IT IS ESSENTIAL TO TAKE NOTE OF THAT NOT DOING AS SUCH MAY IN A REAL SENSE IMPLY THAT YOU ARE PASSING UP THE ENTIRETY OF THE GOOD TIMES.

HOW YOU MIGHT WANT TO MEET AND SPEAK WITH OTHER WEB CLIENTS, PARTICULARLY ONES THAT SHARE SIMILAR PERSPECTIVES AND CONVICTIONS AS YOU DO? TO CONTEMPLATE JOINING AN INTERPERSONAL INTERACTION SITE, ON THE OFF CHANCE THAT

YOU HAVEN'T EFFECTIVELY DONE AS SUCH. WITH REGARDS TO EFFECTIVELY FINDING AND DISCUSSING ON THE WEB WITH OTHER WEB CLIENTS, LONG RANGE INTERPERSONAL COMMUNICATION DESTINATIONS ARE, MAYBE, THE MOST IDEAL WAY TO GO. ASSUMING YOU ARE KEEN ON JOINING AN INTERPERSONAL INTERACTION SITE, THE MAIN THING THAT YOU SHOULD DO IS TRACK DOWN AN ORGANIZATION

TO JOIN. YOU CAN
WITHOUT MUCH OF A
STRETCH OBSERVE
VARIOUS ORGANIZATIONS
BY PLAYING OUT A
STANDARD WEB SEARCH.
FOR THE BEST QUERY
ITEMS, YOU MIGHT NEED
TO LOOK WITH THE WORDS
LONG RANGE INFORMAL
COMMUNICATION OR
INTERPERSONAL
INTERACTION SITES.
IN YOUR HUNT, ALMOST
CERTAINLY, THAT YOU
THINK OF A GENUINELY
HUGE NUMBER OF
VARIOUS

SYSTEMS ADMINISTRATION DESTINATIONS. WELL KNOWN DESTINATIONS THAT MIGHT BE REMEMBERED FOR YOUR LIST ITEMS MIGHT INCORPORATE, YET WON'T BE RESTRICTED TO, MYSPACE, ORKUT, YAHOO! 360, FRIENDFINDER, FRIENDWISE, FACEBOOK, AND CLASSMATES. WHENEVER YOU HAVE SETTLED ON THE CHOICE TO JOIN A SPECIFIC LONG RANGE INTERPERSONAL COMMUNICATION SITE,

WHETHER OR NOT IT IS ONE OF THE ONES REFERENCED ABOVE, YOU SHOULD HAVE TO ENLIST WITH THE SITE. INDEED, EVEN FREE SYSTEMS ADMINISTRATION NETWORKS NECESSITATE THAT YOU GO THROUGH THE ENROLLMENT INTERACTION. WHENEVER YOU ARE ENLISTED, YOU OUGHT TO HAVE THE OPTION TO BEGIN SPEAKING WITH OTHER LOCAL AREA INDIVIDUALS. BEFORE YOU BEGIN CONVEYING,

YOU MIGHT HAVE TO
FOSTER YOUR ONLINE
PROFILE OR PROFILE
PAGE, CONTINGENT UPON
THE SYSTEMS
ADMINISTRATION
WEBSITE BEING
REFERRED TO. DESPITE
THE FACT THAT IT MIGHT
APPEAR TO BE
ADEQUATELY SIMPLE TO
MAKE A PROFILE, THERE
ARE NUMEROUS WEB
CLIENTS WHO ARE
UNCERTAIN PRECISELY
WHAT THEY OUGHT TO
AND OUGHT EXCLUDE.
MAYBE, QUITE POSSIBLY
THE MAIN THING TO

REMEMBER FOR YOUR ONLINE SITE IS YOUR IMAGE. WHILE AN INDIVIDUAL PICTURE IS DISCRETIONARY, IT IS GREAT. NUMEROUS WEB CLIENTS APPRECIATE TAKING TO SOMEBODY THAT THEY CAN FIND TO THEM, WITHOUT A PICTURE THIS IS TROUBLESOME. ASSUMING YOU ARE HOPING TO UTILIZE INTERPERSONAL INTERACTION SITES JUST TO MEET NEW COMPANIONS YOU MAY NOT REALLY NEED TO POST A PRIVATE PICTURE,

YET YOU MIGHT HAVE TO ON THE OFF CHANCE THAT YOU ARE HOPING TO FIND LOVE ON THE WEB. WITH REGARDS TO WEB DATING, NUMEROUS PEOPLE WON'T SEE AN INTERNET BASED PROFILE IN THE EVENT THAT AN IMAGE IS EXCLUDED. NOTWITHSTANDING YOUR PHOTO, YOU MIGHT NEED TO INCORPORATE YOUR NAME.

PRESENTLY, WITH REGARDS TO YOUR NAME, YOU SHOULD BE MINDFUL. YOU ARE PROMPTED AGAINST GIVING YOUR

COMPLETE NAME, PARTICULARLY IN THE EVENT THAT YOUR PROFILE OR PROFILE PAGE CONTAINS AN INDIVIDUAL PHOTO OF YOU. NOTWITHSTANDING YOUR NAME, YOU MIGHT NEED TO PUT DOWN YOUR AREA. SIMILARLY AS WITH YOUR NAME IT IS ESSENTIAL TO SHOW ALERT. YOUR IMAGE, YOUR LOCATION, AND YOUR COMPLETE NAME CAN BE PERILOUS, PARTICULARLY ASSUMING IT FALLS INTO SOME

UNACCEPTABLE HANDS.
HOWEVER MUCH YOU
MIGHT WANT TO FILL
YOUR LONG RANGE
INTERPERSONAL
COMMUNICATION
PROFILES WITH
INDIVIDUAL DATA, YOU
ARE ENCOURAGED TO
CONTEMPLATE YOUR
WELLBEING PRIOR TO
WHATEVER ELSE.
YOU MAY LIKEWISE NEED
TO REMEMBER DATA FOR
YOURSELF. THIS DATA
MIGHT INCORPORATE
YOUR LEISURE
ACTIVITIES, GIVES THAT
ARE ESSENTIAL TO DO,

YOUR PREFERENCES, AND
YOUR AVERSIONS. WITH
NUMEROUS LONG RANGE
INTERPERSONAL
COMMUNICATION SITES,
INCLUDING MYSPACE, YOU
WILL SEE THAT THERE
ARE PRESET PROFILE
FIELDS FOR THIS DATA.
NOTWITHSTANDING
PRESET INQUIRIES OR
CLASSES ON YOUR
DIFFERENT
PREFERENCES, YOU MAY
LIKEWISE TRACK DOWN
EXTRA DATA, INCLUDING
FUN POLLS. NUMEROUS
INTERPERSONAL
INTERACTION SITES

WILL ASK THAT YOU PORTRAY YOUR CHERISHED SHADING, YOUR OBJECTIVES THROUGHOUT EVERYDAY LIFE, YOUR MOST HUMILIATING SECOND, ETC. LIKEWISE WITH YOUR OTHER INDIVIDUAL DATA, IT IS CRITICAL TO REMAIN AS DUBIOUS AND CONCEIVABLE AND NOT UTILIZE ANY COMPLETE NAMES, PARTICULARLY GENUINE ONES.

BY REMEMBERING THE PREVIOUSLY MENTIONED FOCUSES, YOU OUGHT NOT

EXCLUSIVELY HAVE THE OPTION TO MAKE AN INTERNET BASED LONG RANGE INTERPERSONAL COMMUNICATION PROFILE THAT IS LOADED UP WITH SIGNIFICANT DATA, YET YOU CAN DO AS SUCH WHILE REMAINING PROTECTED SIMULTANEOUSLY. YOUR SECURITY ON THE WEB IS IN YOUR GRASP, TO THAT END IT IS CRITICAL TO CONSIDER WELLBEING, JUST AS WEB PROMINENCE.

DO YOU CHERISH
UTILIZING THE WEB TO
MEET AND CONVERSE
WITH NEW INDIVIDUALS?
ASSUMING THIS IS THE
CASE, THERE IS A DECENT
POSSIBILITY THAT YOU
HAVE KNOWN ABOUT
INTERPERSONAL
INTERACTION SITES
PREVIOUSLY.
IN THE EVENT THAT YOU
HAVE NOT, YOU WILL
NEED TO FIND OUT ABOUT
THEM SINCE THEY ARE
QUICKLY TURNING INTO
THE MOST WELL KNOWN
METHOD FOR SPEAKING
WITH OTHERS ON THE
WEB.

IN THE EVENT THAT YOU WEREN'T AT THAT POINT MINDFUL, INTERPERSONAL INTERACTION SITES ARE SITE THAT BASICALLY GO ABOUT AS A WEB LOCAL AREA. WHILE ALL INTERPERSONAL INTERACTION SITES HAVE THEIR OWN PRINCIPLES AND LIMITATIONS, NUMEROUS SITES WORK LIKEWISE, WITH COMPARATIVE OBJECTIVES. THEY WILL LIKELY PERMIT WEB CLIENTS TO ASSOCIATE WITH OTHER WEB CLIENTS ON THE WEB,